UP CLOSE

Snakes

PAUL HARRISON

W
FRANKLIN WATTS
LONDON · SYDNEY

Published in 2007 by Franklin Watts

Copyright © 2007 Arcturus Publishing Ltd

Franklin Watts
338 Euston Road
London NW1 3BH

Franklin Watts Australia
Level 17/207 Kent Street
Sydney, NSW 2000

Author: Paul Harrison
Editor (new edition): Ella Fern
Designers (new edition): Steve West, Steve Flight

Picture credits: Nature Picture Library: 5 top, 7 middle, bottom, 11 top, 18 top, bottom, 20 bottom, 21 bottom, 22, back cover; NHPA: front cover, title page, 2, 3, 4, 5 bottom, 6, 7 top, 8, 9 top, bottom, 10, 11 bottom, 13, 14, 15, 17, 19 top; Science Photo Library: 12, 16, 19 bottom, 21 top.

A CIP catalogue record for this book is available from the British Library

Dewey number: 597.96

ISBN: 978-0-7496-7689-6

Printed in China

Franklin Watts is a division of Hachette Children's Books.

Contents

Snakes Alive

S nakes are members of the reptile family. But they are not just lizards without legs. Snakes can swim and some can even fly.

LAYING EGGS

Most snakes lay eggs. Unlike hens' eggs, snakes' eggs are not hard. They feel soft and leathery. Most snakes are terrible parents. They leave their eggs somewhere warm and let them get on with it.

HOT AND COLD

Like other *reptiles*, snakes rely on the sun to warm them up. When they are warm, they have lots of energy. When the temperature drops, they are less active.

Snakes have scaly bodies but they are not slimy like fish.

SUN AND SEA

Snakes are usually found in the warmer parts of the world where there is plenty of sun. Some snakes live in water, too.

BONY

Snakes get their shape from their very long skeletons. Snakes can have literally hundreds of ribs. Their backbones reach almost all the way down their bodies.

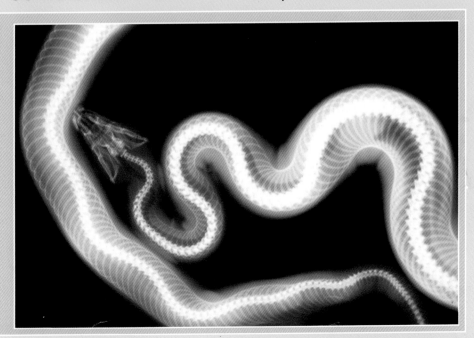

Senses

Snakes can't blink—they don't have eyelids!

A s *predators*, snakes have to catch other animals to live. They use their highly-developed senses to help them spot their *prey*.

SIXTH SENSE

Most animals have five senses—sight, hearing, touch, taste and smell. Some snakes have a sixth sense—heat sensors.

SMELL

Snakes can use their tongues to smell with! This is why their tongues are always popping in and out.

EAR EAR

Snakes can't hear but they feel vibrations in the ground if something is close by.

BOO!

If snakes can't see far enough they lift their bodies up into the air. Then they can peer over the grass to see what's going on.

7

Getting Around

You would think getting around with no arms or legs would be a real problem—but not for a snake! Snakes have lots of ways of getting from A to B.

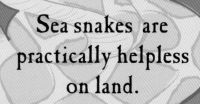

Sea snakes are practically helpless on land.

FISHY

Many underwater snakes have flattened tails to help push them along as they swim.

AIRBORNE

The golden flying snake doesn't bother climbing up and down trees. It launches itself through the air from one tree to the next.

SLITHERY

Snakes slither along the ground by pushing against any lumps and bumps with their belly muscles.

SIDEWINDER

The sidewinder snake has a strange way of getting about. It throws it body across the desert sand in a sideways slither.

Bad Manners

S nakes bite and spit and generally don't have time for good manners.

FABULOUS FANGS

When it bites, a snake's front fangs inject its victims with poison. Some snakes can fold their fangs away when they don't need them!

SPITTING

The spitting cobra can warns off predators by spitting at them. Its poisonous spit causes a burning sensation in the eyes that warns off threatening hunters.

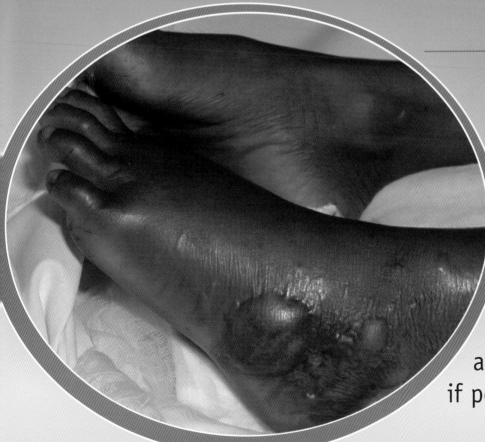

POISON

Snake poison is also called *venom*. It's made up of lots of different *toxins*. Not all toxins hurt humans much, but it's always worth avoiding a snake bite if possible.

MOUTH FULL

Some snakes, such as the egg-eating snake, swallow their food whole. The snake swallows the egg first. Then special teeth inside its gullet break the egg shell so it can digest the nutrients inside. Then it spits out the shell.

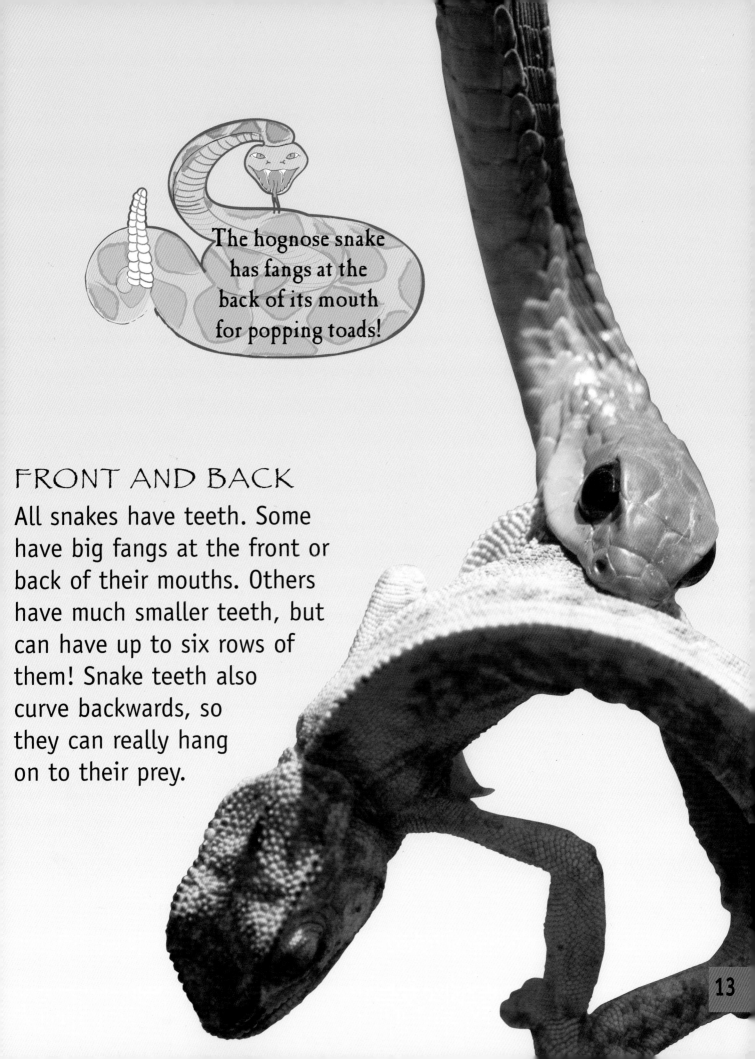

The hognose snake has fangs at the back of its mouth for popping toads!

FRONT AND BACK

All snakes have teeth. Some have big fangs at the front or back of their mouths. Others have much smaller teeth, but can have up to six rows of them! Snake teeth also curve backwards, so they can really hang on to their prey.

Putting the Squeeze

Not all snakes rely on bites and poison to kill their prey. Some snake are called constrictors, which means they squeeze their prey to death with their bodies.

GIANT

The biggest snake of all is the reticulated python. It can grow over 9 metres long. Pythons wait in the trees to *ambush* their victims. Then they wrap their coils around the prey before it can escape.

TINY TERROR

Rat snakes and milk snakes are small *constrictors* that are less than a metre long.

WATERY WONDER

Anacondas are most at home in water. They are found in rivers and lakes in South America and they are big enough to kill a *caiman*.

15

OPEN WIDE

Big snakes need big meals. Pythons and anacondas sometimes kill deer and wild pigs. But these snakes don't chew their food, so how can a python eat a deer? Easy, it unhinges its jaw and swallows the animal whole!

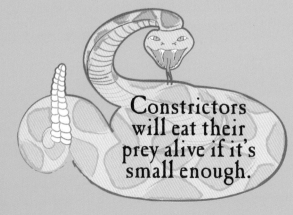

Constrictors will eat their prey alive if it's small enough.

You Have Been Warned

S nakes will always try to avoid fights if they can. If they feel threatened, they use warning signals. They only attack if they have to.

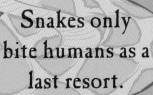

Snakes only bite humans as a last resort.

HOODIES

Cobras have a flap of skin behind the head that they can expand like a hood. This makes them look bigger and more frightening.

17

RATTLE

The end of a rattlesnake's tail is made up of bony material. When a rattlesnake is threatened, it shakes this bony rattle.

DEADLY

Snakes also use colour as a warning device. A very colourful snake like this coral snake is likely to be poisonous. The colour is a warning to predators to back off.

HISS

Noise can be an effective way for a snake to let you know it's not happy. The bullsnake is a master of the threatening hiss.

OPEN WIDE

This Eastern hognose snake opens its mouth wide when attacked. It hisses and rears up to scare off its attacker. Then it pretends to be dead. It rolls over onto its back and lets its tongue hang out. And if the attacker still doesn't leave it alone—it bites!

Man Bites Snake

T he very biggest snakes have no natural predator — except humans. Our species is proving to be a major threat to these fabulous creatures.

Getting venom from a snake is called "milking."

BAD MEDICINE

Traditional medicine uses pieces of chopped up snake as ingredients. However, snake venom can be extracted without harming the snake.

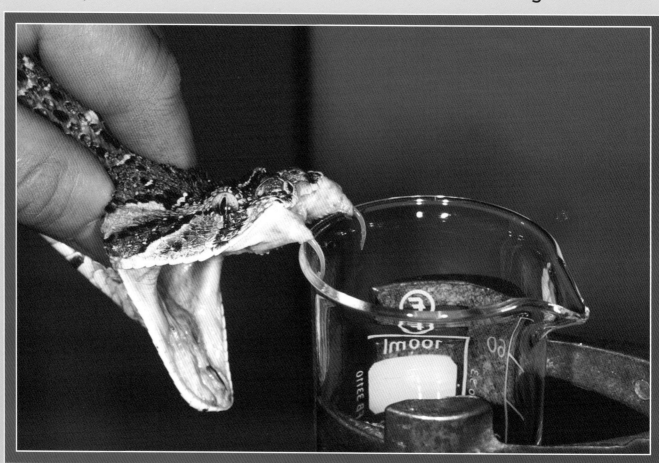

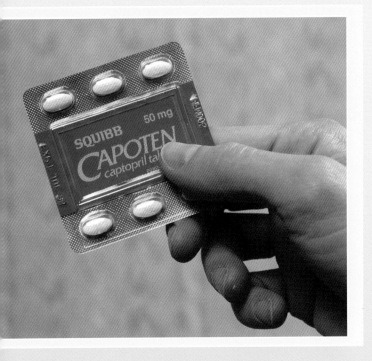

CURE

You might think snake venom would do more harm than good. However, snake venom is now being used to create medicines. It can help fight illnesses including strokes and even cancer.

HUNTING

Snakes will bite when attacked, but they are not a real threat to humans. However, they are still feared and hunted in many places.

SAVE OUR SKIN

Unfortunately for snakes, some people still want their skin to make bags, belts and shoes.

Glossary

Ambush

When a predator lies in wait for its prey. Then it attacks suddenly, taking the prey by surprise.

Caiman

A type of reptile, like an alligator, found in the Americas.

Constrictor

A snake who crushes its prey to death in its coils.

Predator

An animal (a carnivore) that hunts and eats other animals.

Prey

An animal that is hunted by other animals for food.

Reptile

A cold-blooded vertebrate (animal with a backbone), covered in scales or a horny plate. Reptiles include lizards, snakes, crocodiles and turtles.

Toxin

A poisonous substance that can cause reactions and disease.

Venom

The poison that some snakes use when they bite.

Further Reading

The Best Book of Snakes
Christiane Gunzi, Kingfisher, 2003

Slithering Snakes
Lynn Huggins-Cooper, Franklin Watts, 2005

Snakes
Rachel Firth and Jonathan Sheikh-Miller, Usborne, 2001

The Snake Scientist
Sy Montgomery, Houghton Mifflin (Scientists in the Field Series), 2001

I Wonder Why Snakes Shed Their Skin and Other Questions About Reptiles
Amanda O'Neill, Kingfisher, 1996

Index